Homosexuality

and the

Church of England

The position following
'Some Issues in Human Sexuality'

Andrew Goddard

Lecturer in Christian Ethics, Wycliffe Hall, Oxford

GROVE BOOKS LIMITED

RIDLEY HALL RD CAMBRIDGE CB3 9HU

Contents

Acknowledgments

A common refrain in my family at the moment is 'Dad, what are you writing/talking about? Not sex/homosexuality again? Can't you talk about something more exciting!' It is a sentiment I—and I suspect many others in the church—increasingly share. The sad fact, however, is that for much of the last year or so and perhaps for much of this year, this has been the major ethical subject in the Anglican Communion. The statement shows that I must above all thank Lis, Jono and Nell for their patience, support, understanding and their own insights and questions as I have contributed in various ways to this discussion.

   I have also learned an enormous amount from the many people who have shared their views or stories and asked me difficult questions both in private conversations and at public meetings. In particular, the friendship developed in working with Peter Walker, especially on 'True Union in the Body?' which has shaped much of this booklet, has been one of the highlights. He and a number of other friends, including members of the Grove Ethics group, greatly improved the text by reading and commenting on it but should not be blamed for the flaws that remain.

The Cover Illustration is by Peter Ashton

First Impression January 2004
ISSN 1470-854X
ISBN 1 85174 552 1

Setting the Scene

1

That Was the Year That Was

Throughout 2003 the Church of England and Anglican Communion appeared to enter self-destruct mode, focussed on homosexuality. In May, Canada's New Westminster diocese witnessed the first authorized Anglican blessing of a same-sex union within days of Anglican Primates agreeing 'we as a body cannot support the authorization of such rites.' At the same time as that primatial meeting Canon Jeffrey John was announced as Bishop of Reading-designate.[1] As opposition to that appointment grew, leading to his withdrawal on 6th July, New Hampshire elected (on 7th June) Canon Gene Robinson as bishop, a divorcee living openly in a sexual relationship with another man. ECUSA's General Convention approved that election and carried a motion that 'local faith communities are operating within the bounds of our common life as they explore and experience liturgies celebrating and blessing same-sex unions.'[2] An emergency Primates' Meeting was called and after two days, on 16th October, unanimously agreed that the actions in North America 'threaten the unity of our own Communion as well as our relationships with other parts of Christ's church, our mission and witness, and our relations with other faiths…and polarize Christian opinion.' They warned Robinson's consecration would 'tear the fabric of our Communion at its deepest level.' Within hours it became clear ECUSA's Presiding Bishop would ignore such warnings and, on 2nd November, he consecrated Gene Robinson. Two days later, with surprisingly little media attention, the Church of England's House of Bishops published *Some Issues in Human Sexuality: A Guide to the Debate*.

> *The Anglican Communion appeared to enter self-destruct mode*

Some Issues—A Summary

The 358-page report came from a Working Party (chaired by the Bishop of Oxford) as the House of Bishops' response to a 1997 General Synod motion that commended their 1991 report *Issues in Human Sexuality* for discussion. It is, 'a guide to the debate' and 'a discussion document' clearly stating that although in the Church of England 'there is a range of views on homosexuality'[3] there are 'two official statements' (9.1—numbers in brackets refer

3

to paragaphs in *Some Issues*): the last synodical expression of the mind of the Church as a whole'[4] and *Issues* that expresses 'the theological position and pastoral practice of the House of Bishops' and so 'has considerable authority within the Church' (9.1.3). The guide represents neither a tightening nor a loosening of church teaching or policy. It works within the parameters of *Issues* and 'does not seek to change the position of the House of Bishops from the one expressed there.'[5] It aims 'above all…to bring about greater levels of mutual understanding, encouraging us not only to be better informed but to listen to one another with genuine hearing and imaginative insight.'[6] As the *Companion to Some Issues in Human Sexuality* explains,[7] the guide has three sections.

Part One—The Background to the Current Debate
The first three chapters lay the historical, biblical and theological founda-tion. The opening chapter sketches wider society's debates and developing Anglican thinking in other areas (such as contraception) that reveal a com-mon pattern in which the Church has reasserted traditional Christian principles while allowing the outworking of these to be shaped by pastoral realities and dilemmas (1.2.62–65). It acknowledges the Church could change its position on homosexuality but only 'providing that (a) it had sufficient theological grounds for so doing and (b) that such a change did not entail a change to its core ethical beliefs' (1.5.2). In contrast to three earlier Church reports (none supported by Synod) that 'were prepared to consider the pos-sibility that homosexual activity might be regarded as morally justifiable in certain circumstances' (1.3.13) the guide is based on *Issues* where 'there is no suggestion that the choice of a same-sex relationship is morally justifiable' (8.4.60).

Chapter two addresses the use of the Bible in sexual ethics, laying down hermeneutical principles given the Bible 'is regarded by Anglicans…as the living word of God by means of which we may learn about the salvation that God offers to us and how we should live in the light of that salvation' (2.1.6). It steers between a belief that we create texts' meaning and a belief that we can certainly establish a final, fixed determinate meaning. It calls for humility and charity faced with different interpretations and for recognition that all readings are partial and provisional. Everyone brings experiences and presuppositions to the text but the text must be free to challenge these as it 'is only as we respect the freedom of the text that we respect the free-dom of God to speak to us through his word' (2.7.12). The chapter stresses the need to interpret particular texts in light of the Bible as a narrative of salvation history witnessing to God's grace and guiding discipleship.

Chapter three outlines a biblically rooted Trinitarian theology of sexuality (3.4.29–48) to show why 'according to both the mainstream interpretation of

4

the Bible and Christian tradition, the proper context for sexual relations has been and is a permanent and exclusive relationship of love between two people of the opposite sex' (3.5.4). It concludes by examining some critiques of traditional teaching that nevertheless remain committed to orthodox Trinitarian and incarnational theology.

Part Two—The Nature of the Current Debate
The central four chapters introduce various debates by outlining arguments for and against positions. Chapter four examines biblical teaching on homosexuality. It explains the 'traditionalist' understanding of key texts and outlines 'revisionist' critiques concluding that 'at the moment, the traditional understanding of these passages remains the most convincing one in the minds of most biblical scholars' (4.4.34). The strongest challenge to traditional understandings is chapter five. This surveys the rise of the gay movement and scholarly debates concerning gender and sexual identity with a particular focus on lesbian feminist theologies. Chapter six addresses bisexuality, raising questions concerning sexual orientation and identity and the role of experience in interpreting and challenging biblical and traditional teaching. The seventh chapter provides an excellent survey of different Christian attitudes to transsexualism—the experience that one's physical anatomy is incompatible with one's true sexual identity and the possible resolution of this by sex reassignment surgery.

Part Three—Responding to the Current Debate
Chapter eight discusses homosexuals, bisexuals (8.5) and transsexuals (8.6) in the life of the Church. It defends *Issues* (8.4.83) against those who argue for no policy (8.4.2–5), for a stricter policy (8.4.6–19), and for a more 'inclusive' policy (8.4.20–82). The final chapter seeks to structure and guide the church's debate amidst diversity over sexual morality. It proposes four things the church cannot do (9.6.1–19):

- ignore diversity;
- say there is no objective scale to compare views;
- claim differences are superficial;
- claim sexual conduct is not important,

and five things it must do (9.6.20–62):

- ask about the scope of legitimate diversity;
- ask how to achieve a common mind;
- be honest about effects on our unity;
- be willing to act in line with beliefs;
- beware of ignoring the Spirit.

More Than An Issue...

Some Issues is a wide-ranging, well-researched guide that will hopefully shape the debate over coming months and years. That debate cannot, however, be only an academic one or a political one driven by defence of party lines. A major problem arises when discussion is purely political and not pastoral and personal, when it takes place *about* people and 'issues' rather than genuinely *with* the people most directly concerned. In recent years I have got to know a number of gay Christians and Christian groups that, from differing perspectives, offer support. Jeremy Marks (Courage), Martin Hallett (TfT), Colin Coward (Changing Attitude) and the internet community of Bridges Across have all taught me a great deal I could never have learned from debates or reading books, even the Bible.[8] Perhaps nobody brought this home to me more than my personal tutor at Cranmer Hall, Michael Vasey. Michael was writing *Strangers and Friends*[9] at the time and his words during the last Synod debate on this subject bear repeating as we enter this new stage:

> The Church is a place of danger for gay people. The two attempts in my life to out me as a gay person were by substantial Evangelical leaders. In the first attempt three people who are now diocesan bishops in this room were silent partners. The Church is dangerous to gay people. I have lived my life in the Evangelical movement and I can tell from within it that you do not understand us as gay people and that you have offered me in my life no viable strategy for ordering my life.[10]

If we are to have a Christian discussion, those of us for whom the 'issues' are not directly personal—the overwhelming majority—must take time to get to know gay Christians. In the words of Stephen Fowl,

> It should not, then, be the responsibility of homosexual Christians to provide 'narratives of homosexual holiness'…The onus is on other Christians who may enter (or have already entered) into friendships with homosexual Christians…[11]

The 'listening to the experience of homosexual persons' called for by Lambeth 1998 must be genuine and not limited to those who agree with us. The media and most 'revisionists' give the false impression that all gay Christians are 'revisionist.' Meanwhile, many 'traditionalists' only listen to gay people who agree with them.[12] There would perhaps be less heat and greater light if every time anyone criticized a viewpoint they thought of a gay Christian they personally knew and respected who sincerely believed that the view being critiqued was God's call or command.

Two Commitments

This booklet is driven by two commitments which many believe to be in tension: firstly, a strong commitment to traditional Christian teaching in this area; and secondly a conviction that 'the debate about human sexuality…is not one that is going to go away. Furthermore, *it is not a debate that should go away*' (1.5.1, italics added). It therefore explains and defends the position found in *Issues* and the 1998 Lambeth Resolution but in such a way that understanding and dialogue is encouraged with those who disagree.

Rather than discussing 'homosexuality,' I plan to examine five areas: homosexual *conduct* and the biblical texts (chapter 2), homosexual *desire* and homosexual *identity* and the claim that contemporary knowledge requires us to rethink the tradition (chapter 3), homosexual *relationships* and homosexual *unions* and the argument that once 'homosexuality' is reconnected to love then a more affirmative Christian stance is possible and necessary (chapter 4). Although this structure is not that of Some Issues, reference will frequently be made to relevant paragraphs of the report. The aim throughout is to expound traditional views, respond to criticisms, and raise issues for 'revisionist' responses. The final chapter examines the current debate and asks what is needed if the church is to approach it constructively and remain united. But there is an essential task of scene-setting to be done before we can move on to any of this.

A Christian Vision of Sexuality

It is vital to grasp the larger Christian vision of sexuality before focussing on homosexuality. 'Traditionalists' do not only hold their view because of a handful of biblical texts. Those texts cannot be detached from the larger biblically-based traditional understanding of sexuality. *Some Issues*, before addressing biblical texts on homosexuality, therefore rightly sketches a theology of sexuality as one criterion for judging whether the church should alter its position on homosexuality (8.4.82).

The bishops sum up mainstream Christian thinking by reference to C S Lewis's statement, 'Either marriage, with complete faithfulness to your partner, or else total abstinence' (cited at 1.2.1). This is based on 'a core of [five] commonly held beliefs about human sexuality' (1.2.4). Unless they can convincingly integrate their reassessment of homosexuality within this traditional Christian vision of sexuality, 'revisionists' must also present an alternative vision of human sexuality.

'Traditionalists' do not only hold their view because of a handful of biblical texts

1 Scripture and Sexuality

'The first belief is that God's intention for human sexual activity has been made known to us primarily in Holy Scripture' (1.2.5). One reason sexuality debates are so passionate is that this belief appears to be ignored or over-turned by many in the light of social pressure or personal experience. *Some Issues* warns that 'suggesting that our moral intuition is to be the judge of Scripture rather than the other way round...goes against the theological approach...traditionally accepted by the Church of England' (4.4.70). Indeed, if the Church went down this route 'it would be difficult to see how this would be compatible with the affirmations of the authority of the Bible that have been a consistent feature of the Anglican tradition and the Anglican formularies, and it would mean that the Church of England had departed in this respect from the orthodox Christian tradition' (4.4.71).

The bishops' discussion of bisexuality highlights the difficulties that must arise if Scripture is subordinated to experience, socially accepted norms or alleged new scientific insights:

Obviously...in practice there is a constant interplay between experi-ence and biblical interpretation. Nevertheless...it would be difficult to see how it would be consonant with the Anglican theological tra-dition to give the last word to personal experience. The Bible has to provide the framework within which to interpret our experience rather than the other way around (6.4.3).

2 Male and Female

Secondly, on the basis of Genesis 1 and 2, Christians hold that 'the division of humankind into two distinct but complementary sexes is not something accidental or evil but is, on the contrary, something good established by God himself when he first created the human race' (1.2.9). This created order of humanity made in God's image as male and female undergirds Christian approaches to homosexuality.

In relation to what it ultimately means to be human, the St Andrew's Day Statement rightly states, 'there can be no such thing as "a" homosexual or "a" heterosexual; there are human beings, male and female, called to redeemed humanity in Christ.' As Oliver O'Donovan has written:

This...marks a limit upon what the Church can, with any integrity, contemplate. If it is asked to adopt some alternative myth of creation-order to replace that in which Adam acclaims Eve as 'bone of my bone and flesh of my flesh,' it can only refuse.[13]

3 Marriage

Thirdly, as is clear from Christ's appeal to Genesis in the gospels, marriage is part of God's good ordering of creation: 'God ordained that men and women should relate to each other in marriage for the three reasons classically expressed in the marriage service of the BCP' (1.2.12). Those three reasons or goods are procreation, a remedy against sin, and mutual society, help and comfort.

Currently this understanding is widely lacking in society and often missing or distorted in much Christian thinking. Marriage is commonly understood in terms of a human contract between two individuals who have 'fallen in love.' It is then easy to understand why 'gay marriage' may be considered possible and desirable. The Christian understanding, however, sees marriage not only in terms of a relationship but as an institution created and established by God.[14]

4 The Goodness of Sex

Fourthly, even when virginity was highly exalted and parts of Christian tradition struggled with a positive account of sexual desire and sexual intimacy, the Christian understanding was that 'sexual union has a legitimate place in the context of marriage' (1.2.14). The church is not 'anti-sex' and does not equate sex with sin. It does, however, have a clear understanding of a proper ordering of sexual desire and conduct.

5 Marriage, Singleness, Abstinence and Celibacy

Fifthly, because sexual activity has its proper setting within marriage, Christians have held 'that those who were not married should not engage in any sexual activity at all and that those who were should engage in it only with their spouse' (1.2.19). Within this understanding the church has recognized that God may call some to the specific vocation of celibacy (based on the examples of Jesus, Paul and Christian ascetics and biblically rooted in Matt 19.10–12 and 1 Cor 7). The call to celibacy is 'a witness that we belong to the world to come, in which attachments to particular individuals will be transcended in a universal relationship of love to all' (3.4.101). It is 'a way of life in which some people are called to offer themselves wholly to God in a lifelong commitment' (3.4.102).

It is essential celibacy is not equated with chastity, singleness or abstinence

It is essential celibacy is not equated with chastity, singleness or abstinence. *Chastity* is the calling of all, taking different shape in the two forms of life God established: faithfulness within marriage and abstinence outside it. *Singleness* is 'a provisional state in which the individual concerned is open to the possibility of marriage' whereas *celibacy* 'is a state of life in which the

9

possibility of marriage has been renounced, often on a permanent basis.' Singleness 'may well be a simple matter of circumstance' whereas celibacy 'is something that is chosen' (3.4.103). *Abstinence* is the form of chastity for all who are single whatever the reason for their singleness. This terminology must be recovered in the current discussion.

The Church understands sexual activity not as a basic human right but as a good tied by God to his good gift of marriage. The disciplines of marital faithfulness are expected of those not married in a church ceremony. The disciplines of abstinent singleness are expected even of those who do not take vows of celibacy. The challenge is for churches to be communities that nurture chastity by supporting marriages and by encouraging the growing number of single people (including those attracted to people of the same sex) to live lives of abstinence.

Conclusion

These five beliefs generate 'the Christian sexual ethic as this has been understood down the centuries by the mainstream of the Christian tradition' (3.5.8). It is this Christian vision and not just Christian teaching on homosexuality that is so alien and unpopular in most of contemporary Western society. It is this that is fundamentally under question in current debates on homosexuality as 'homosexual activity has been consistently condemned within the Christian tradition… because of the five core beliefs about human sexuality' outlined here (1.2.25). If homosexual activity is accepted then these five core beliefs must also be to some degree revised.

If homosexual activity is accepted then these five core beliefs must also be to some degree revised

The bishops cite Norman Pittenger, Eugene Rogers and Rowan Williams as examples of those who believe that 'a Trinitarian and incarnational theology should lead us to accept and even celebrate same-sex sexual relationships' (3.6.34). Such a move, however, requires either a convincing critique of the traditional account and a credible alternative Christian vision of sexuality or a persuasive case that a positive understanding of same-sex sexual relationships is compatible with the five principles sketched above.

Homosexual Conduct and the Bible 2

The case that Scripture condemns all homosexual conduct is well rehearsed in many places, both briefly[15] and in full.[16]

Some Issues chapter four provides an accessible guide to the key texts and debates.[17] In what follows I summarize the traditional understanding and respond to seven common 'revisionist' questions.

Traditional Reading of Scripture

The traditional reading of biblical teaching on homosexuality has three bases. *First*, biblical texts referring to homosexual conduct are consistently negative. If one asks whether the biblical writers disapprove of those same-sex activities *to which they refer*, then 'the answer is a straightforward and uncontroversial "Yes."'[18] 'Revisionist' Walter Wink admits that 'Simply put, the Bible is negative towards same-sex behaviour, and there is no getting around it.'[19] This uniform biblical witness distinguishes homosexuality from other areas of dispute (such as women's leadership) where varied emphases exist within Scripture.[20]

Second, the texts appear in Old and New Testaments and a variety of biblical genres. Whether in Old Testament narrative (Gen 19 on Sodom) or law (Holiness Code of Leviticus 18 and 20) or New Testament theology (Romans 1) or apostolic moral exhortation (1 Cor 6 and 1 Tim 1) we repeatedly find God's people—Israel and the church—warned against homosexual conduct.

Third, this fits the bigger biblical picture of human sexuality and the wider biblical drama. The *creation* of humanity shows the significance of being male and female and the divinely ordained norm of marriage between a man and a woman. Homosexual conduct is then understood, most explicitly in Romans 1, as one sign of humanity's *fall*. When God redeems a holy people, his Law—in contrast to the pattern of life in neighbouring nations—explicitly condemns homosexual conduct in *Israel*. *Christ* himself lives a faithful life of abstinent singleness and teaches clearly on sexual morality. When *the church* then includes Gentiles, sexual immorality is prohibited (Acts 15) and the apostle to the Gentiles teaches that homosexual conduct is unacceptable (4.3.73-82).

This reading is not naïve, fundamentalist proof-texting. It is the plain sense of the biblical text and of its bigger story in regard to sexuality. It is the consistent understanding of two thousand years of Christian biblical inter-pretation and the official position of the Church of England, the Anglican Communion and the wider Christian church. Although the claim Scripture speaks against all homosexual conduct has been questioned, 'the herme-neutical principles set out in Chapter 2 [of *Some Issues*], and the consensus of biblical scholarship, still point us in the direction of the Church's traditional reading of the biblical material' (4.5.1).

*Question One: Can it not be shown that the texts are negative about **some** but not **all** homosexual conduct?*
This objection follows a common tactic faced with 'difficult' biblical texts: each text is isolated and individually re-interpreted. The most susceptible text is one that has shaped much Christian thinking—Genesis 19. Most now accept that the desire 'to know' the visitors has sexual intent but the sexual intent (never accomplished) is 'gang rape.' Most 'traditionalists' therefore acknowledge that Genesis 19 on its own therefore has little *direct* bearing on current debates, although it shows God's judgment on sexual sin (4.2.14).

The same may be thought true of texts (such as Deut 23) referring to cultic prostitution. This misunderstands their context. In the ancient world this was the most acceptable form of homosexual conduct so 'anyone rejecting homosexual prostitution would, therefore, be rejecting homosexuality *per se*' (4.2.37). It is difficult to limit the texts from Leviticus to cultic homosexuality—nothing implicit or explicit in the text suggests this and other sexual prohibitions are universal—but were such a limit to be accepted, then the same argument applies here also.

Debate continues over two key New Testament terms (*arsenokoitai* and *malakoi*) used in 1 Cor 6 and 1 Tim 1. Some restrict these to cultic, promiscuous or adult-boy forms of homosexual conduct. Although undoubtedly common forms of same-sex behaviour in the ancient world, these were not the only forms. In his general lists of sins, there is no evidence Paul only had *some* forms of same-sex conduct in mind. On the contrary, there is strong evidence Paul coins his original term *arsenokoitai* from the Levitical prohibition about 'lying with a man' and so intends it to be comprehensive (4.3.28-29, 35-37). It also seems that in 1 Timothy his list is related to the Decalogue and classes homosexual conduct as a sin against marriage.

Finally, there is Romans 1. Some read this in terms of individual biography and claim it does not apply to non-idolaters or those who do not abandon natural relations with women but only ever enter same-sex relationships. But Paul is giving a wider portrayal of godless society and culture, not a psychological account of individual sexual attraction. He is showing that, when humanity rejects God, our societies are handed over to certain patterns of life. Many Christians in the Global South find this directly relevant to Western churches—devoted to idols of materialism, consumerism, and self-gratification our society is similar to the decadent empire based in Rome when Paul wrote Romans. Furthermore, Paul's allusions to Genesis, his use of 'nature' language and his inclusion of female homosexual conduct strongly suggest a fundamental dis-ordering of the proper creation order between men and women; a wrong image of God (idolatry) leads to a wrong reflection of God's image in sexual relationships (immorality). He is showing that the exchanges in v 26ff are repeating the basic error of v 25: they are telling a lie rather than the truth. In other words, all sexual acts between people of the same sex—even in a loving, faithful relationship—do not tell the truth about who the people are as men or women or the truth about the reason God made us as sexual beings for the joy of sexual union.

In summary, the arguments for limiting the scope of the negative texts are mainly special pleading. Furthermore, even if they were held to be persuasive in all cases, Scripture would then be silent. Nobody has claimed any biblical text is affirmative about homosexual conduct and so a more positive Christian moral judgment would have to be based on other grounds than Scripture.

Question Two: Is the Bible not silent about faithful, loving same-sex relationships?

This is true if one approaches Scripture with a narrow, literalistic mindset. If, however, one reads the text intelligently, then two problems arise. Firstly, one must show that all the biblical prohibitions are not universal and therefore inapplicable in loving relationships. Secondly, granted a silencing of the traditional texts, one must show *why* such relationships would be acceptable given Scripture's overall witness. The big picture of biblical teaching about sexuality points to a negative Christian judgment about homosexual conduct *even without specific texts on the subject*. While 'mutual love' and 'covenantal faithfulness' are commended in Scripture, they are never commended as sufficient to justify a *sexual* relationship outside of marriage. As chapter four shows, this explains the consequent confusion among advocates of change concerning what same-sex sexual relationships can be approved.

Question Three: We are not literalists with other texts of Scripture, so why with homosexuality?

The focus of this complaint is the popular argument that Christians conveniently ignore the prohibitions of Leviticus by eating shrimps and black pudding, cutting beards and wearing polycotton shirts (Lev 11, esp v 10; 19.19, 26-27). This fails to recognize that the traditional view is not based only on two texts in Leviticus. Furthermore, applying this part of Leviticus and not others is not random. It derives from wider well-established rules of Christian interpretation such as the distinction between moral, civil and ceremonial law. Those wishing to disregard Leviticus on homosexuality still generally wish to appeal to its command to love one's neighbour as oneself (Lev 19.18, between the two texts on homosexuality) or the Jubilee principles of debt relief (Lev 25), not to mention commands against bestiality and incest (also Lev 18 and 20). They must therefore develop a new alternative method of reading and applying Old Testament law to show why Christian tradition has erred in accepting Leviticus' rejection of homosexuality.

Question Four: What does Jesus says about homosexuality?
It is strictly true that the gospels lack any explicit reference to homosexuality. It has, however, never been a principle of good biblical interpretation that if Jesus cannot be cited then the church can do whatever it believes best. We would then judge idolatry an open question as Jesus is silent on that! All arguments from silence are precarious, particularly when the silence is only that of the gospels and the rest of Scripture speaks consistently and clearly.

In this case, evidence suggests silence supports the traditional view. First, Jesus' teaching on sexual conduct is, if anything, stricter (on adultery in the heart and on divorce) than the Old Testament and his Jewish contemporaries. Second, in Jesus' day the Law was understood to prohibit all homosexual conduct. Homosexual acts would therefore automatically be included in Jesus' rejection of sexual immorality (*porneia*, Mark 7.21). Third, Jesus challenged widely held misconceptions about what God required but we have no record that he said something like, 'You have heard that it was said a man shall not lie with a man as a woman but I say to you that when the men are expressing covenantal love they are blessed.' As the bishops state, 'It is therefore impossible to conceive that Jesus would have endorsed homosexuality had this been an issue that had arisen during his ministry' (4.3.63).

Question Five: If we reject the Bible's reasons for objecting to homosexual conduct then why can we not reject its negative conclusions?
This raises an important question as to how far we can know the rationale behind the biblical commands and whether disagreement with that rationale can sanction rejection of the command. Certainly, some *historic* Christian arguments against homosexual practice (such as its non-procreativity) must be revised or rejected in the light of current Christian understandings. It is, however, far from clear that the same applies to *biblical* texts.

Various claims have been advanced as to *why* the Bible speaks against homosexual conduct. These include the failure to produce children within Israel (but how does that relate to the New Testament?), taboos concerning mixing and uncleanness (but Paul does not view the texts in this way), or the objection to men being passive or women being active in sexual intercourse (for which no biblical but some cultural evidence can be cited). There is therefore no agreement on the allegedly flawed reasoning behind the command.

There is, in fact, one clear and obvious biblical rationale for its negative statements: that homosexual conduct is one sign of humanity's rejection of God's creation purpose for those made in his image as male and female. This is derived from the standpoint of the canon as a whole and that of particular texts. It is most explicit in Romans 1: creation reveals something to us of who God is (vv 19–20); humans reject God and instead exalt creation to be our god (vv 21–23); God therefore gives us over to actions which degrade our created bodies (v 24) and as part of that we exchange the way God made us to relate sexually for something that is against nature (vv 26–27).

Question Six: Surely other biblical texts and biblical principles such as 'inclusion' should be given weight in our judgment on homosexuality?
'Revisionists' rightly draw attention to the covenantal love between David and Jonathan and to Jesus' welcome of those treated as outcasts and condemned as sinners. Bigger biblical themes such as love of neighbour and liberation of the oppressed must also shape Christian thinking. It would, though, be wrong to assume these automatically point in one direction— 'Exodus' is the name of a 'traditionalist' group seeking to help people to be 'liberated' from their homosexuality'!

Recently 'inclusion' and texts such as Acts 15 have been highlighted.[21] This important biblical theme is however incapable of providing guidance on sexual conduct. All agree we need an 'inclusive' church. All agree this does not mean abandoning all moral norms that might exclude people. The question is therefore what norms apply. The argument from inclusion takes an important strand in Scripture but it cannot yield an account of the demands of Christian discipleship. To support 'revisionist' conclusions it must smuggle in a particular, ontological understanding of homosexuality (critiqued in chapter three). It then appears to assume that there is a human right to sexual expression which is given a 'Christian' form by reference to the need for sexual relationships to exhibit marital qualities. None of these controversial (and usually implicit) steps can be derived from 'inclusivity.'

Question Seven: If the church has changed its understanding in other areas and either revised or rejected scriptural teaching might not the Spirit be leading us to do the same here?
This reminds us that, until Christ's return, all our understanding is provisional. We must therefore display humility and charity towards those with whom we disagree and 'be open to the possibility of revising our reading in

the light of our own study of the text in new contexts or on the basis of fresh insights provided by other readers' (2.2.25). The fact that the church is continually to be reformed and has changed its understanding on taking interest, contraception, divorce and remarriage and the role of women means we must be open to revision in this area. The church must therefore continue to wrestle with these issues rather than ignore them or silence debate by the use of power.

However, because the church has changed its mind on some issues does not mean it must change it on this one. 'Wrong on slavery, wrong on women, therefore wrong on homosexuality' has rhetorical power but is intellectually flawed. In particular, the claim that other revisions occurred because the church rejected the teaching of Scripture is a distortion of the processes involved. Appeals to the Spirit's leading which set God's Word and God's Spirit in opposition are fundamentally flawed.

As Acts 15 shows, any radical steps need to be weighed and accepted by the wider church before they can be declared the work of God. When the worldwide church remains convinced that traditional teaching is faithful to Scripture it is therefore more likely that the spirit of the age not the Spirit of God is animating those who claim to be 'prophets.'

Conclusion

In relation to homosexual conduct it is therefore clear that 'the various suggestions for revising the traditional view of the biblical material have not succeeded in changing the consensus of scholarly opinion...At the moment, the traditional understanding of these passages remains the most convincing one in the minds of most biblical scholars' (4.4.34).

There are, however, two further arguments: (1) that we know better than the Bible because of our understanding of homosexual *desire* and *identity* and (2) that the church today must provide a constructive pattern of sexual conduct for gay people by commending homosexual *relationships* or *unions*. Anyone with a high view of biblical authority and convinced Scripture condemns all homosexual conduct will not be easily persuaded by these claims. They must still hear, understand and weigh the arguments. Those unconvinced that Scripture supports the traditional view and those willing to argue that 'compatibility with Scripture is not the only consideration' (4.4.54–71) may find these arguments more persuasive.

Homosexual Desire and Identity 3

For many people the strongest 'revisionist' argument is that we now have an understanding of homosexuality that requires revision of traditional teaching.

This is often expressed in terms of homosexual orientation and its biological causation. Rather than starting with the language of 'orientation,' I begin with the traditional Christian and biblical language of 'desire' before examining, in a discussion of 'identity,' the complex question of what is meant by 'orientation' and the claim to 'be gay.'[22]

What Causes Homosexual Desire?

Why people experience same-sex sexual attraction—often expressed in terms of nurture versus nature—is highly controversial. It is also unclear whether a definitive answer would help the moral debate. Many argue that although deeper understanding might require different pastoral responses, scientific findings alone cannot determine Christian moral teaching. Just as other actions considered sinful (such as excessive alcohol consumption) remain wrong whatever the causes, so any explanation as to why certain sexual desires are formed is incapable of determining whether such desires are disordered or true to God's creational purpose for humanity (4.4.66).

Most 'revisionists' seek to establish homosexuality as biologically based. A number of different claims have been made in recent years focussed on genes, hormones and brain size.[23] None has yet been proved or gained widespread acceptance in the scientific community. Edward Stein's careful analysis concludes,

> The scientific study of human sexual desire is, at best, going through a period of revolution...A decade or so from now, the emerging research program might turn out to have been a false start in the search for an account of how human sexual desires develop.[24]

The same uncertainty applies to psychological theories. These have also taken various forms, with claims related to early sexual experience, family dynamics (especially relationships with the same-sex parent), and failure to conform to childhood gender expectations. In contrast to biological theories, these are increasingly out of favour in secular academic study. Stein again helpfully sums up:

> Although there is little evidence for any specific experiential or psychological theory, experience and environmental factors seem likely to be relevant in some ways to explaining the development of the complex psychological dispositions that we call sexual orientations.[25]

Rather than a single cause for homosexual attraction, a multi-causation model is increasingly plausible. This would mean that the form and strength of each person's same-sex desire has a distinctive, perhaps unique, mix of biological and psychological factors, and it may be better to speak of 'homosexualities.' This leads into the next controversial question.

Can Homosexual Desires Be Changed?

Especially in North America, many 'traditionalists' use the language of 'healing' homosexuality and offer 're-orientation.' They invest in a psychological causation whereas opponents look for biological bases for homosexual desire.

The fundamental difficulty here is a lack of extensive, careful, balanced enquiry into the different programs of therapy, counselling and Christian ministry. Instead, there is reliance on testimony from different people but this is strong on both sides.[26] It is irrefutable that some people ('ex-gays') claim significant changes in the pattern of their sexual desires away from homosexual desire, in some cases sufficient to enter a stable marriage. It is also beyond dispute that many sincerely and intensively seek such change, often at great personal cost, but find their sexual desires remained unaltered or, in some cases (ex-ex-gay), a belief they have changed proves false. This latter experience recently led the evangelical group *Courage* to rethink its whole understanding and ministry and so leave the Evangelical Alliance.

If diverse biological and psychological factors lie behind experiences of homosexual desire then this pattern of change is unsurprising. A consensus may now be emerging that change is neither entirely impossible nor as easy or common as some 'traditionalists' imply. In their study of science and homosexuality, 'traditionalist' Christians Jones and Yarhouse state, 'we do not share the optimistic and seemingly universal generalization of some conservative Christians who seem to imply that anyone with any motivation can change…'[27] They warn that 'it appears to us that profound change of orientation occurs infrequently.'[28] Robert Spitzer, having been very sceptical to claims for 'change' and having no Christian 'agenda,' has recently claimed that some highly motivated individuals, using a variety of change efforts, can make substantial change in multiple indicators of sexual orientation and achieve good heterosexual functioning (see www.newdirection.ca/research/spitzer.htm).

Theologically, Christians must beware of investing in a particular outcome in this particular debate. If homosexual desires are a sign of our fallen humanity then there may be signs of God's redemption here and now. There is, however, no ground for demanding or expecting this in any particular case. Pastorally, it is crucial that a clear distinction is made between experience of homosexual desires and the choices made in response to such desires. Christians must not buy into a deterministic approach that leaves us enslaved to our desires. However, to expect those with homosexual desires to undergo 'therapy' or 'ministry' is unnecessary and often harmful. Those who constantly pursue 'change' here may need to discover God's redemptive presence in their lives by other means.

The Moral Status of Desires

There is a tendency sometimes to take the existence and strength of homosexual desire in some people as proof such desires are not wrong. This denies the power of sin. As the Book of Common Prayer reminds us, one way we sin is that we 'follow too much the devices and desires of our own hearts.' In a statement that would arouse outrage were it not from a gay atheist, Matthew Parris exposes a flaw in this argument: faced with the argument 'God cannot reject any loving impulse He has implanted in men,' Parris confesses he wants to ask, 'Really? How about child-molesting?'[29]

The argument that we must accept desires appears plausible because the usual language is that of 'orientation.' This is then understood as something true about the person at the deepest level of their being. This leads into discussion of *homosexual identity* and the constructionist/essentialist debate.

What is Sexual Orientation?

The first important point is that 'orientation' need not match conduct because each person's orientation 'crucially involves his or her dispositions and desires.'[30] It is therefore possible, whatever one's 'orientation', to abstain from sexual conduct (as Christian tradition expects of all who are unmarried) or to act in a way that does not reveal the 'orientation' ('straight men' engaging in homosexual conduct in prisons or 'gay men' marrying to conform). Two crucial questions are how one measures 'orientation' and what we are referring to by 'orientation.'

In the popular mind, sexual orientations come in two forms—homosexual and heterosexual—with an occasional acknowledgment some may be 'bisexual.' However, most researchers in this area acknowledge greater complexity with at least a spectrum from exclusively heterosexual to exclusively homosexual (as in Kinsey's 0–6 scale).[31] This greater complexity and potential fluidity in 'orientation' presents a major challenge to widely and uncritically held common assumptions.

Whatever measure of 'orientation' is used, the even more important question is what sort of thing an 'orientation' is and why we might say of someone 'he is a homosexual' or 'she is a heterosexual.' Stein illustrates this by reference to a fictional world called Zomnia. People there identify themselves as either 'fronters' or—though there are fewer of this persecuted and widely misunderstood group—'backers.' These labels refer to their 'sleep orientation,' that is, whether they sleep on their backs or stomachs. Nobody disputes most people tend to sleep in one of these two ways. We, however, do not use and are unlikely to adopt, the categories of 'fronter' and 'backer' no matter how important they are to Zomnians. This is despite the fact that it would be possible to apply such categories in our society. We do not do this in part because we do not think how people sleep is of great importance. But, more seriously, we do not believe that 'sleep orientation' is a trans-cultural or natural category that helpfully distinguishes between different kinds of human beings. We see it as either meaningless or as a particular social categorization which has a role (for good or ill) within Zomnian culture but is not universally applicable to all humans in all societies. In short, a 'backer' identity is a social construction and not something essential to humankind. In relation to 'sleep orientation' we are social constructionists and not essentialists.

The key question is how to understand claims in our culture for a homosexual identity. Is 'sexual orientation' simply a social construct so that to speak of 'homosexuals' in Ancient Greece or modern Nigeria is as meaningless as a Zomnian speaking about 'fronters' in contemporary England? Or is 'sexual orientation' something—like blood group—that people in all societies have even if they do not know about it or name it?

This whole discussion is often ignored or falsely treated as equivalent to the nature/nurture debate about the causation of homosexual desire. It is, however, of increasing significance in the church debate. Most (though not all) 'revisionists' are essentialists. They believe sexual orientation identifies a basic natural sub-section of humanity that the church must now recognize and so revise its teaching on sexual ethics. If grace perfects nature then we need to ask what it means to perfect a homosexual nature. In contrast, many 'traditionalists' are social constructionists. Their strong theological grounds are that the only created distinction within humanity of relevance to sexual ethics is that between male and female. There are two sexes—male and female—not four (gay, lesbian, straight man, straight woman) or more. To say otherwise has no basis in Scripture or Christian tradition. Given the highly contested nature of the contemporary constructionist/essentialist debate, the church therefore has no authority to identify or address people as essentially 'homosexuals' and 'heterosexuals' in its account of what it means to be human and its sexual ethic.

Conclusion

To claim that we know much more about homosexuality than previous generations underestimates the historical breadth of awareness and overestimates our contemporary knowledge. With a few exceptions, the overriding 'revisionist' assumption is that an essentialist and biologically based understanding of homosexuality is firmly established. 'Revisionists' then conclude that 'traditionalists' must be treating homosexuals as in some sense inferior or inherently more sinful and disordered than heterosexuals, and that Christian tradition makes demands of homosexuals that are practically impossible given their 'nature.' The challenge for such 'revisionists' is to scrutinize their assumptions and to develop a consistent theological understanding of what it is to be human. They must then show that they are not implicitly accepting a strong determinism if they claim the church must offer a structure of relationships in which one's 'orientation' can be expressed and an account must be given of what this means for 'bisexuals.'

The major challenge for 'traditionalists' is to listen and respond to the biographical testimonies of gay Christians used in 'revisionist' understandings of homosexual desire and identity. They must also offer a theological and historical deconstruction of the contemporary 'gay identity' which has gained so much popular credibility. Only then can they find ways of expressing traditional teaching and exercising pastoral care that can be understood in a culture that has uncritically imbibed essentialist conceptions of sexual orientation.

As Oliver O'Donovan has written (cited in *Some Issues* 1.5.4),

> Our first and last duty in this sphere is to discern the light the gospel sheds on the Gay movement of our time. The church must learn to attest its faith in the gospel before this cultural phenomenon. The gay Christian must learn to attest the truth of the gay self-consciousness in the light of the gospel. What we commit ourselves to, when we commit ourselves to true debate is no more and no less than this learning.

4

Homosexual Relationships and Unions

The other main 'revisionist' argument is that 'traditionalists' falsely abstract homosexual conduct out of loving human relationships. Once we avoid this error (it is said), then we can discern and establish structures within which homosexual conduct is morally acceptable and to which biblical prohibitions do not apply.

What Sort of Relationship?

One of the greatest difficulties in the current debate is that 'revisionists' are far from clear as to the form of relationship the church should commend. Some react against the 'oppression' of traditional teaching with a stress on 'liberation' that apparently rejects any strong moral framework. The Lesbian and Gay Christian Movement Statement of Conviction states 'it is entirely compatible with the Christian faith not only to love another person of the same sex but also to express that love fully in a personal, sexual relationship.' Leaving aside this libertine approach, three models for same-sex relationships have been proposed. Firstly, there are appeals to 'friendship' (for example, Michael Vasey and Elisabeth Stuart) that often insist that same-sex relationships are different from opposite-sex relationships and so it is wrong to impose a 'marriage' model. Second, writers such as Eugene Rogers extend the traditional language of marriage to embrace same-sex relationships. Third, others such as Jeffrey John hold similar views but dislike using the language of 'marriage.' They propose a third way of life for same-sex couples alongside marriage and singleness that is quasi-marital in form and may be termed a 'covenantal union' or 'same-sex partnership.'

'Revisionists' are far from clear as to the form of relationship the church should commend

There is, therefore, as yet no agreed alternative Christian vision once the traditional call for abstinence outside marriage between one man and one woman is rejected. This 'revisionist' confusion highlights a real danger: can the church responsibly change its traditional teaching and practice before agreeing what forms of sexual same-sex relationships it would accept?

Friendship?

Reflection on friendship is common in writing on homosexuality and a good case can be made that the modern West has lost the gift of true friendship, especially among men. One of the most original and potentially significant parts of *Some Issues* is therefore its discussion of a Christian vision of friendship (3.4.29–48). The difficulty with this strand of 'revisionist' thinking, however, is its claim that sexual expression is acceptable within friendship. Of course, on a broad understanding of 'sexual' there can be 'a legitimate sexual dimension to all relationships of friendship, since they are about reaching out to transcend our loneliness' (3.4.44). There are also, however, limits to affectionate physical contact between friends. Christians have held that the total self-giving of sexual union between friends is a denial of the open, non-exclusive character of friendship that fundamentally distinguishes it from marital union. For the church to legitimate sexual friendships would be to baptize the sexualization of our culture.

The difficulty with this strand of thinking is its claim that sexual expression is acceptable within friendship

The church may, however, offer support and guidance to the growing number of single people in our society (including those who identify themselves as homosexual) by exploring this area further. If 'there can be physical expressions of love by Christians that are manifestations of holiness' (3.4.47) and friendship has 'spiritual significance' then

> One of the things that the Church needs to consider is how it can give public recognition to the importance of friendship. As a number of writers have pointed out, in the past the Church celebrated the importance of same-sex friendships with rites that gave them an official standing. What needs to be explored is what kind of recognition would be appropriate today, and how we might incorporate into our liturgical life an affirmation and celebration of the value of friendship (3.4.39).

In contrast to most liturgies blessing same-sex unions (8.4.48–63), these rites could not commend sexually active friendships, would need to distinguish friendship from marriage and could not exclude future marriage. With these important caveats, this is potentially a creative avenue of exploration in the current church debate.

Marriage?

Accepting same-sex relationships as 'marriage' might appear the most 'conservative' 'revisionist' response because it upholds C S Lewis' summary of the Christian sexual ethic. In fact, it does this by a radical revision of 'marriage' that amounts to its dissolution.

First, including same-sex couples within marriage detaches marriage from Scripture's male-female nuptial imagery and the biblical account of Genesis to which Christ appealed in his teaching. Second, same-sex marriage removes from marriage the otherness of male and female. This destroys the biblical imagery of marital union as a form of re-union in which the two become 'one flesh.' The coming together of one man and one woman in marriage is theologically significant as it witnesses to God's creation purpose in making us male and female. It also symbolizes the Creator's covenant with his creation that is *other* than him. The joining of one man and one woman in marriage provides the most concrete and material sign that we grow in self-knowledge through relationships in which we experience that which is distinctly other than ourselves rather than through that which is fundamentally the same as us. In a fallen world, the reconciliation of opposites is both a gift and a task given by God through his redemption of us in Christ and this is symbolized in the union of male and female within lifelong faithful marriage. This bigger picture about the significance of 'otherness' also explains the centrality of nuptial imagery in Scripture and is essential to the portrayal of marriage as a type of the relationship between God and his people.

Same-sex marriage removes from marriage the otherness of male and female

Third, to treat same-sex couples as married makes openness to the gift of new life an accidental rather than essential feature of God's gift of marriage. Although most Christians now accept that not every sexual act must be open to life and the procreative good within marriage is no longer prioritized, to redefine marriage so that its intrinsic relationship to the gift of children is removed marks a major innovation.

This makes openness t the gift of new life an accidental rather than essential feature of God's gift of marriage

Quasi-marital Covenantal Partnership?

The third option is a new path of holy living apart from marriage or abstinent singleness. Unfortunately, neither Scripture nor tradition support any sexual relationship other than marriage. A new *theological* account is therefore needed as to the nature of this relationship if it is neither part of God's good gift to us in creation nor a personal call bearing witness to the kingdom of God. There are also difficulties with defining such a form of life. Many look to marriage as the model but this presumes marriage's structure and disciplines can be detached from its created male-female structure and applied to sexual relationships between people of the same sex. Appealing to the pattern of divine love in Christ fails to acknowledge that this pattern should be displayed—in different ways—in all human relationships and not simply in sexual bonds between two people.

This proposal's rationale is that it seeks to legitimize homosexual conduct while acknowledging this cannot be done within 'friendship.' It therefore claims the covenantal form of marriage is required to justify sexual expression in a loving same-sex relationship. The difficulty is neither Scripture nor tradition reveal any form of same-sex

It is also unclear how closely the marriage model is to be followed

relationship in which the couple's mutual love can legitimately be expressed through sexual conduct. It is also unclear how closely the marriage model is to be followed, particularly in relation to the exclusivity of the bond. Language of 'faithful' and 'stable' is commonly found with ambiguity as to what these concretely entail. Andrew Yip's study of gay male Christian couples found 70% did not have sexually exclusive relationships. Even among those who expected their partnership to be sexually exclusive, almost half were not and unfaithfulness began within six months to two years of the start of their relationship.[32] Some see here a sign of serious practical problems in expecting the disciplines of marriage within same-sex sexual relationships and even claim that, given the non-procreative nature of sexual activity in such relationships, the commitment to life-long exclusivity is unnecessary.

Same-sex Unions?

At present there are Christians in sexual same-sex *relationships* whose self-understandings embrace all three options discussed above. As yet, official recognition and liturgies for such relationships—which would establish them as publicly defined *unions*—are rare and highly controversial (8.4.35–72). Some Christians are eager to encourage such developments in the name of 'inclusivity,' provision of pastoral care and support, and a distinctive witness to the patterns of sexual behaviour in the wider gay community. Apart from the damage to church unity, other difficulties must be addressed before the Church could officially recognize such unions.

First, the Church would need to clarify how such unions related to traditional teaching. For most, both for and against, such unions entail a radical revision or rejection of that teaching. For some, however, same-sex unions are consistent with upholding the belief that 'homosexual relationships fall short of God's ideal' (8.4.1 cf 1.4.8).

Secondly, the Church would need to decide which of the three models it was embracing and why it was doing so. Unofficial liturgies exist for all three patterns but most are theologically vacuous and unless the Church permitted a totally DIY approach it could not officially sanction such diversity.

Thirdly, the Church would be publicly commending more than one form of sexual relationship. It would ask individuals to choose for themselves whether to submit to the disciplines of Christian discipleship with someone of the same sex or the opposite sex. Instead of understanding itself to have received a *divine promise* and *command* for all human beings, the Church would be offering each person a *personal choice* between possible sexual relationships.

Fourthly, rather than proclaiming the distinction and sexual ordering of male and female within humanity, a new norm would be established alongside or above this and based on the highly contested concept of sexual orientation. This would further confuse many, especially young people, and raise a host of pastoral and theological problems: Should clergy enquire whether the couple really have the orientation their proposed union suggests? If a marriage comes to an end, are people free to switch and choose a same-sex union for their next partnership?

The desire to support gay people and to acknowledge the good in gay relationships is laudable and necessary. For the church to authorize such unions creates major problems. It may make sense in postmodern Western society with its emphasis on individual freedom, self-fulfilment and personal choice but represents a fundamental reconfiguration of Christian moral theology and the understanding of being human. The words of Wolfhart Pannenberg are, in this light, not as surprising or extreme as they appear to many on first reading:

> Here lies the boundary of a Christian church that knows itself to be bound by the authority of Scripture. Those who urge the church to change the norm of its teaching on this matter must know that they are promoting schism. If a church were to let itself be pushed to the point where it ceased to treat homosexual activity as a departure from the biblical norm, and recognized homosexual unions as a personal partnership of love equivalent to marriage, such a church would stand no longer on biblical ground but against the unequivocal witness of Scripture. A church that took this step would cease to be the one, holy, catholic, and apostolic church.[33]

The Church, the Homosexuality Debate and Grace 5

The Surface Issues

The questions raised by blessing same-sex unions have already been discussed. There are two other 'flash-points': ordination and episcopal dissent.

Some Issues strongly defends *Issues'* alleged 'double standard' requiring abstinence from gay clergy but accepting lay same-sex partnerships (8.4.28–34). There is not a double standard. The Church has one standard for sexual relationships: life-long, heterosexual marriage. It applies this standard by a stricter pattern of clergy discipline because of the limited form of discipline on lay Christians and the clergy's obligations within holy orders to uphold Christian teaching and be good examples. As no clergyperson is perfect it would be wrong to pry into their most intimate relationships and remove even those whose sins are not a cause of scandal. However, it is also wrong for clergy to engage in sexual activity outside marriage or to live openly in violation of the Church's teaching.

The objection is *not* to 'gay clergy' but rather to clergy in any non-marital sexual relationship, especially those who are openly so and thereby commend what the Church calls sin. The bizarre claim that this penalizes honesty forgets that an honest response to sin can only take the form of penitent confession. The Church could decide that clergy sexual conduct is unimportant or accept the incoherence of clergy openly violating its teaching in their lives. Unless it does so, the Church must agree a new sexual ethic *before* accepting clergy in sexual same-sex partnerships.

Perhaps a more serious threat to unity lies with episcopal dissent from Church teaching. A minority of bishops are not personally convinced the Church's teaching and practice is right. How does the Church live with this in a time of debate and discernment? Three areas must be distinguished: personal beliefs, public teaching and official actions. It would be wrong and impractical to insist a bishop must personally be fully convinced of the Church's teaching in this area. Difficulties arise when personal doubts become public or several bishops share the same doubts. Such bishops are torn between their calling to teach and uphold the faith and the need for honesty in the Church debate. The collective responsibility largely upheld under Archbishop Carey is increasingly fragile and 'traditionalists' must now develop responses to 'revisionist' bishops. Commitment to serious Church deliberation appears to require greater liberty for bishops to argue 'revisionist' viewpoints (at least in certain contexts). Otherwise, there is no leadership in the debate and suspicions grow that the House of Bishops will one day privately decide the 'present teaching' is the 'past teaching.' However, public pronouncements will increase tensions and impair communion with 'traditionalists'.

What will certainly deepen division is bishops undermining official teaching by their actions. *Some Issues* calls for us 'to be willing to act in accordance with our beliefs.' It is clear that this 'is also true for the Church of England as an institution' (9.6.48). One of the reasons the current situation is so difficult is past hypocrisy and duplicity. That cannot continue—stated policy must be implemented if there is to be any integrity in the continuing discussion.

Getting Under the Surface

One interesting question is 'why homosexuality is such a divisive issue in the Church today' (8.4.84) when other differences are managed more easily. At least two *emotional* or *psychological* reasons cannot be ignored. Firstly, issues of sexuality touch us all at a deep level. For many there is a visceral reaction against homosexuality. This is found on both 'sides' even if 'traditionalists' tend to attract the 'homophobia' label. Secondly, great fear exists. 'Revisionists,' especially if they are themselves gay (particularly gay clergy), fear the 'traditionalist' reaction if they are open and honest. Many 'traditionalists' fear changes will destroy their understanding of Christian faith and make it impossible to remain Anglicans. Given the lack of agreed procedures for change they also fear that revision will occur by gradual compromises, private episcopal agreement or unilateral actions. In recent conversations among the most interesting comments made to me by 'revisionist' friends have been 'What are you frightened of losing and what will show you've lost?' and 'You evangelicals know if you lose this one then your whole view of biblical authority is destroyed—this is your last ditch.'

As this last comment shows there are also deep theological disagreements under the surface here. In addition to differences over Scripture and its relationship to other sources of knowledge, varied understandings of such matters as the effect of sin on humanity as God's good creation, the role of the Spirit in tradition and innovation, the importance of intuition and emotion in true self-understanding, the understanding of 'death to self' and 'self-acceptance', and the relationship of love to moral rules also shape people's responses to questions of sexuality. In many cases, knowing someone's theological stance in areas such as these will enable an accurate assessment of how sympathetic they are to 'traditionalist' and 'revisionist' views on homosexuality before addressing any of the issues discussed in this booklet.

It is because these deeper issues are involved that people on each 'side' can go so far as to see others proclaiming a 'different gospel' in relation to this issue.

Finally, the question of the relationship between Church and society is important. This relates in part as to how in a post-Christendom situation the established church should respond to social change if its traditional stance risks it becoming more like a 'sect'. More specifically, different Christian responses to the shift from a modern to a post-modern culture shape not only the conclusions in debates about sexuality but also how that debate is structured. Division over sexuality may simply bring to the surface these deeper differences. It is therefore unsurprising when people on each side see this as a 'gospel' issue with a 'different gospel' being proclaimed by others.

Living Together?

If theological differences are that deep then some form of institutional realignment to enable expression of diversity may be necessary. To discern whether that is the case or, preferably, to find ways of hospitality, mutual correction, and deeper understanding within the same ecclesial structures, the church must consider what it means to be a community of grace.

Forgiving Grace

'Forgive us our sins as we forgive those who sin against us.' Whatever the differences concerning the language of 'sin' in relation to sex, there is agreement that the gospel's heart is God's defeat of sin and forgiveness of us. There is also increasing awareness how easily we fall into sins of factionalism and schism. Lies, insults and accusations are easily hurled at fellow Christians—'homophobe,' 'fundamentalist,' 'unbiblical,' 'sodomite.' Instead of 'interpretative charity,' resort is made to caricature and distortion of others' viewpoints. Power is abused in order to silence, intimidate or sideline those of different views. Specks are removed from others' eyes while beams remain in our own. We must therefore ask whether in this debate there is in fact 'an unhealthy obsession with sexual sin that prevents people focussing on other forms of sin that are also important' (8.4.84). But we can only do that if we are willing to show and receive God's forgiving grace ministered to us by those whom he has also called into fellowship with his Son.

Welcoming Grace

'Welcome one another, therefore, just as Christ has welcomed you, for the glory of God' (Rom 15.7). There have recently been angry statements about not being able to live in a Church with evangelicals or with gay couples. There has also been a recognition that different parts of the Church have lived in their own sub-cultures and had little genuine fellowship with each other. Jesus reveals a pattern of welcome and inclusion that must take shape in the Church if this debate is to be more than a fight-to-the-death trench warfare between opposing forces.

Unless care is taken there will be *de facto* division into congregations upholding traditional teaching but with few gay people within them and congregations attracting gay people but embracing 'revisionist' views. Finding ways of genuinely welcoming those with whom we differ is, therefore, a priority and essential for real dialogue and progress. In particular, 'traditionalists' must consider how to 'welcome and accept sexually active homosexual people'[34] rather than building barriers to their presence. Upholding the traditional Christian understanding does not entail rejecting those who do not share or live by it. Rather 'the very fact of God's grace means that the Church is summoned to be a welcoming community in which all who seek to follow Christ in the path of discipleship may find unconditional love and support' (9.7.6). Unless and until all parties in the Church can genuinely welcome each other with the welcome they have received from Christ the debate will be sterile rather than creative.

Transforming Grace
'And all of us, with unveiled faces, seeing the glory of the Lord as though reflected in a mirror, are being transformed into the same image from one degree of glory to another; for this comes from the Lord, the Spirit' (2 Cor 3.18). When there is genuine welcome and mutual forgiveness there will be transformation of attitudes, beliefs and forms of debate. Perhaps we divide into camps and attack rather than welcome each other because real transformation would not be in our control and makes us insecure. I may become something I do not currently want to be if I commit myself to listen and to learn. I may find I do not need to stand firm where I currently find myself. As long as we see change as defeat or compromise instead of trusting God's sovereign transforming grace to shape our lives, then we condemn ourselves to changing others' attitudes so they conform to our own.

Costly Grace
'If any want to become my followers, let them deny themselves and take up their cross and follow me' (Mk 8.34). To forgive and be forgiven, to welcome and to be transformed is not cheap but costly. *Some Issues* ends with reflections on costly grace. It challenges us that 'the Christian calling is to follow the path of costly grace, for it is to this path that we are summoned by our baptism into Christ's death and resurrection' (9.7.4).

Costly grace is not for only one group. For example, any church that proclaims traditional teaching on abstinence must make costly choices about its common life if it is to enable and assist those who bear that cross in our sex-obsessed society. In the last year, Archbishop Rowan Williams and Jeffrey John made costly decisions to preserve church unity and enable this debate to continue rather than appear to be short-circuited. What, in the years ahead, does 'denying oneself,' taking up one's cross and following Christ mean for the 'evangelical self' and the 'gay self'?

Conclusion

There will always be people in the Church whose deepest human love is for someone of the same sex. Whether or not they identify themselves as 'gay' or 'lesbian,' they have sadly often found the Church is not a place of grace for them but rather, in Michael Vasey's words, 'a place of danger.' As long as that is the case the gospel is not being obeyed and the Church needs to keep asking itself where it is in error. That is why this question cannot and must not be ignored. That is why the debate must proceed but must also change its tone and focus unless it is to lead to scandal and schism.

It would, however, be wrong to think that the traditional vision of human sexuality is the root cause of this genuine problem. That vision presents a challenge to all of us, whatever our sexuality and perhaps that needs to be more openly acknowledged both in the Church and wider society. Its strong biblical basis has been demonstrated here and is reaffirmed by the House of Bishops in *Some Issues*. Any church claiming to be guided and ruled by the Word of God cannot dismiss or ignore that scriptural foundation. The challenge to it based on the contemporary 'gay identity' must be heard and weighed but that identity is itself open to serious questions from both secular and Christian perspectives. The alternatives offered to abstinent singleness are varied but all face serious theological—and often pastoral and practical—problems if they are claimed to present a viable Christian strategy for the ordering of people's lives. Given the strength of the traditional sexual ethic and the weaknesses in 'revisionist' critiques, the Christian church need not be ashamed of what she believes nor cower when her vision of sexuality and its conclusions about homosexual conduct no longer conform with society's sexual mores.

Nevertheless, Vasey's challenges remain to those of us who believe it wrong to abandon the wisdom of Scripture and two millennia of Christian tradition: Will we work so that the Church is not 'dangerous to gay people'? Will we really seek to understand gay people? Will we create Christian communities in which our vision becomes reality and so is not a harsh law but embodied as the gospel of grace? Will we establish a Church where recognition and support are given to single people and chaste loving friendships and it is demonstrably no longer the case that gay Christians can legitimately say 'you have offered me in my life no viable strategy for ordering my life'?

Notes

1. The Primates' Meeting also discussed and commended to the Communion *True Union in the Body?* which explores in more detail some of the material that follows in this booklet and is available from Grove Books www.grovebooks.co.uk

2. Resolution C051 passed by General Convention 2003.

3. Three views sketched at 1.4.6–9, 9.2 and 9.3 explore diversity within the Church of England and Anglican Communion.

4. 9.1.2. This motion states, 'This Synod affirms that the biblical and traditional teaching on chastity and fidelity in personal relationships is a response to, and expression of God's love for each one of us, and in particular affirms (1) that sexual intercourse is an act of total commitment which belongs properly within a permanent married relationship, (2) that fornication and adultery are sins against this ideal, and are to be met by a call to repentance and the exercise of compassion, (3) that homosexual genital acts also fall short of this ideal, and are likewise to be met by a call to repentance and the exercise of compassion, (4) that all Christians are called to be exemplary in all spheres of morality, including sexual morality, and that holiness of life is particularly required of Christian leaders.' It was carried 403–8 with 13 abstentions.

5. Foreword by Bishop of Oxford, p ix.

6. *ibid.*

7. *Companion* (Church House, 2003) is a 23–page booklet summarizing the key points of *Some Issues* and providing questions for reflection and discussion.

8. The groups are on the web: www.courage.org.uk; www.truefreedomtrust.co.uk; www.changingattitude.org; www.bridges-across.org

9. Michael Vasey, *Strangers and Friends*, Hodder and Stoughton, 1995.

10. General Synod, *Report of Proceedings*, July Group of Sessions (1997) p 351.

11. Stephen Fowl, *Engaging Scripture*, (Oxford: Blackwell, 1998) pp 121–2.

12. All categorisations in this debate are dangerous and potentially misleading. Here 'traditionalist' refers to those who adhere to the Christian vision of sexuality discussed below and 'revisionist' to those who seek to revise this, especially to accept certain forms of homosexual conduct.

13. In Timothy Bradshaw (ed), *The Way Forward?* (SCM, 2nd edn, 2003) p 30.

14. On the institution of marriage see Oliver O'Donovan, *Marriage and Permanence* (Grove Ethics No 26), especially chapter 1. For a more recent account of traditional Christian teaching see Christopher Ash, *Marriage* (IVP, 2003).

15. Mark Bonnington and Bob Fyall, *Homosexuality and the Bible* (Grove Biblical booklet B 1).

16. Robert A.J. Gagnon, *The Bible and Homosexual Practice: Texts and Hermeneutics* (Nashville: Abingdon Press, 2001).

17. The key texts (with relevant paras of discussion in *Some Issues*) are Gen 19.1–14 (4.2.2–15), Lev 18.22 and 20.13 (4.2.16–29), Deut 23.17–18 (4.2.30–50), Rom 1.24–27 (4.3.2–23), 1 Cor 6.9–10 (4.3.24–32) and 1 Tim 1.10 (4.3.33–55).

18. Walter Moberly, 'The Use of Scripture in Contemporary Debate About Homosexuality', Theology, 103 (July/August 2000).

19. Wink in *Christian Century* and at *www.pts.edu/gagnon6.html*

20. R.T. France, *A Slippery Slope? The Ordination of Women and Homosexual Practice: A Case Study in Biblical Interpretation* (Grove Biblical booklet B 16). William J. Webb, *Slaves, Women & Homosexuals: Exploring the Hermeneutics of Cultural Analysis* (Downers Grove: IVP, 2001).

21. For fuller discussion of this see my *God, Gentiles and Gay Christians* (Grove Ethics booklet E121).

22. This area is discussed in a number of places in *Some Issues*, especially 1.1.8, 4.4.58-66, chapter 5 (especially 5.3.31-33) and 6.2.5-6.

23. Chandler Burr, *A Separate Creation: How Biology Makes Us Gay*, (London: Bantam Press, 1996).

24. Edward Stein, *The Mismeasure of Desire: The Science, Theory and Ethics of Sexual Orientation* (Oxford: OUP, 1999) p 228.

25. Stein, *Mismeasure*, p 257.

26. *Some Issues* helpfully includes personal voices from different perspectives at the opening of chapters 4, 7 & 8.

27. Stanton L. Jones & Mark A. Yarhouse, *Homosexuality: The Use of Scientific Research in the Church's Moral Debate* (Downers Grove: IVP, 2000) p 148.

28. *ibid*, p 182.

29. *Times*, 9th August, 2003.

30. Stein, p 70.

31. See Stein, ch 2.

32. Andrew Yip, 'Gay Male Christian Couples and Sexual Exclusivity.' Sociology 31 (1997) 2: 289-306

33. Article in *Christianity Today*, 11th Nov 1996.

34. ACUTE, *Faith, Hope & Homosexuality: A Report*, (London: Evangelical Alliance, 1998).